Lexile: _AD240L_

AR/BL: _2.0_

AR Points: _0.5_

Subtracting with Sebastian Pig and Friends On a Camping Trip

By Jill Anderson

Illustrated by Amy Huntington

Series Math Consultant:
Cassi Heppelmann
Elementary School Teacher
Farmington School District
Minnesota

Series Literacy Consultant:
Allan A. De Fina, Ph.D.
Dean, College of Education / Professor of Literacy Education
New Jersey City University
Past President of the New Jersey Reading Association

Enslow Elementary
an imprint of

Enslow Publishers, Inc.
40 Industrial Road
Box 398
Berkeley Heights, NJ 07922
USA

http://www.enslow.com

To Parents and Teachers:

As you read Sebastian's story with a child,

    *Rely on the pictures to see the math visually represented.

    *Use Sebastian's notebook, which summarizes the math at hand.

    *Practice math facts with your child using the charts at the end of this book.

Enslow Elementary, an imprint of Enslow Publishers, Inc.

Enslow Elementary® is a registered trademark of Enslow Publishers, Inc.

Copyright © 2009 by Enslow Publishers, Inc.

Library of Congress Cataloging-in-Publication Data
Anderson, Jill, 1968-
  Subtracting with Sebastian pig and friends : on a camping trip / written by Jill Anderson ; illustrated by Amy Huntington.
    p. cm. — (Math fun with Sebastian pig and friends!)
  Includes index.
  Summary: "Review basic subtraction with Sebastian Pig"—Provided by publisher.
  ISBN-13: 978-0-7660-3361-0
  ISBN-10: 0-7660-3361-9
  1. Subtraction—Juvenile literature. I. Huntington, Amy, ill. II. Title.
QA115.A533 2009
513.2'12—dc22
                2008028471

Editorial Direction: Red Line Editorial, Inc.

Printed in the United States of America

10 9 8 7 6 5 4 3 2 1

To Our Readers: We have done our best to make sure all Internet Addresses in this book were active and appropriate when we went to press. However, the author and the publisher have no control and assume no liability for the material available on those Internet sites or on other Web sites they may link to. Any comments or suggestions can be sent by e-mail to comments@enslow.com or to the address on the back cover.

Enslow Publishers, Inc. is committed to printing our books on recycled paper. The paper in every book contains 10% to 30% post-consumer waste (PCW). The cover board on the outside of every book contains 100% PCW. Our goal is to do our part to help young people and the environment too!

Table of Contents

Sebastian Pig and his friends are going camping. But some things are missing. Help Sebastian use subtraction to find the answer. Need a hint? Look in Sebastian's notebook. Look at the pictures, too. Can you spot who may be taking things?

7

Let's Go!

What a great place to camp!

"What should we do first?" asks Patty Porcupine.

Paddles Anyone?

"Let's go for a ride!" Sebastian says.

Oh no! There should be three paddles. But there are only two. How many are missing?

Sebastian subtracts. He opens his notebook. He writes the bigger number first. "What is three take away two?" he says. Aha! One paddle is missing.

What other math problems use 3, 2, and 1? Sebastian makes a list.

$$3 - 2 = 1$$

Fact family:
3 - 1 = 2
1 + 2 = 3
2 + 1 = 3

Putting Up the Tent

It's time to put up the tent. Where are the pegs to hold it down?

There should be four pegs. But there are only two. How many are missing?

Hungry for Hot Dogs

Patty Porcupine wants to eat. She looks for the hot dogs.
There were five hot dogs. Now there are only two.
How many are missing?

13

5 - 2 = 3

Fact family:
5 - 3 = 2
2 + 3 = 5
3 + 2 = 5

A Noisy Night

It's time for bed. The campers get their earplugs. Sebastian cannot find his earplugs.

There were six earplugs. His friends are using four.
How many are missing?

6 - 4 = 2

Fact family:
6 - 2 = 4
2 + 4 = 6
4 + 2 = 6

Where Are the Worms?

In the morning, the friends go fishing.
Patty counts the worms.

There were seven worms. Now there is just one!
How many worms are missing?

$$7 - 1 = 6$$

Fact family:
7 - 6 = 1
6 + 1 = 7
1 + 6 = 7

18

Not Enough Eggs

Next comes breakfast. Milo needs eight eggs. But there are just three eggs left. How many are missing?

Milo cooks the three eggs with lots of bread.

ALL YOU CAN EAT!
25¢

8 - 3 = 5

Fact family:
8 - 5 = 3
5 + 3 = 8
3 + 5 = 8

Who Took the Markers?

After breakfast, everyone goes for a walk. Patty does not want to get lost. She ties nine orange markers along the way.

Patty picks up the markers on the way back. She can only find five. How many are missing?

9 - 5 = 4

Fact family:
9 - 4 = 5
4 + 5 = 9
5 + 4 = 9

22

10 - 1 = 9

Fact family:
10 - 9 = 1
9 + 1 = 10
1 + 9 = 10

Only One Ice Pop

At camp, Milo yells, "Ice pops!"

There were ten ice pops in the box. But Milo sees
just one. How many are missing?

Where Is the Corn?

Patty makes corn for dinner. She had 12 ears of corn. Now there are only four ears. How many ears of corn are missing?

12 - 4 = 8

Fact family:
12 - 8 = 4
8 + 4 = 12
4 + 8 = 12

Missing Marshmallows

Sebastian goes to get a bag of marshmallows. Where is it?

"One bag of marshmallows minus one bag of marshmallows equals ZERO BAGS OF MARSHMALLOWS! How could anybody do this?"

1 - 1 = 0

Fact family:
1 + 0 = 1
0 + 1 = 1

Sebastian feels a tug on his shorts. He looks down. There are the marshmallows! There is the paddle! There are all the missing things!

"We are sorry," the mice say. "We were only having fun."

Everyone is happy! Everyone eats the marshmallows. There is enough for everyone.

Now You Know

You helped Sebastian keep track of all his missing things. These charts will help you keep track of more subtraction problems.

- 0

$1 - 0 = 1$
$2 - 0 = 2$
$3 - 0 = 3$
$4 - 0 = 4$
$5 - 0 = 5$
$6 - 0 = 6$
$7 - 0 = 7$
$8 - 0 = 8$
$9 - 0 = 0$
$10 - 0 = 10$
$11 - 0 = 11$
$12 - 0 = 12$

- 1

$1 - 1 = 0$
$2 - 1 = 1$
$3 - 1 = 2$
$4 - 1 = 3$
$5 - 1 = 4$
$6 - 1 = 5$
$7 - 1 = 6$
$8 - 1 = 7$
$9 - 1 = 8$
$10 - 1 = 9$
$11 - 1 = 10$
$12 - 1 = 11$

- 2

$2 - 2 = 0$
$3 - 2 = 1$
$4 - 2 = 2$
$5 - 2 = 3$
$6 - 2 = 4$
$7 - 2 = 5$
$8 - 2 = 6$
$9 - 2 = 7$
$10 - 2 = 8$
$11 - 2 = 9$
$12 - 2 = 10$

- 3

$3 - 3 = 0$
$4 - 3 = 1$
$5 - 3 = 2$
$6 - 3 = 3$
$7 - 3 = 4$
$8 - 3 = 5$
$9 - 3 = 6$
$10 - 3 = 7$
$11 - 3 = 8$
$12 - 3 = 9$

- 4

$4 - 4 = 0$
$5 - 4 = 1$
$6 - 4 = 2$
$7 - 4 = 3$
$8 - 4 = 4$
$9 - 4 = 5$
$10 - 4 = 6$
$11 - 4 = 7$
$12 - 4 = 8$

- 5

$5 - 5 = 0$
$6 - 5 = 1$
$7 - 5 = 2$
$8 - 5 = 3$
$9 - 5 = 4$
$10 - 5 = 5$
$11 - 5 = 6$
$12 - 5 = 7$

- 6

6 - 6 = 0
7 - 6 = 1
8 - 6 = 2
9 - 6 = 3
10 - 6 = 4
11 - 6 = 5
12 - 6 = 6

- 7

7 - 7 = 0
8 - 7 = 1
9 - 7 = 2
10 - 7 = 3
11 - 7 = 4
12 - 7 = 5

- 8

8 - 8 = 0
9 - 8 = 1
10 - 8 = 2
11 - 8 = 3
12 - 8 = 4

- 9

9 - 9 = 0
10 - 9 = 1
11 - 9 = 2
12 - 9 = 3

- 10

10 - 10 = 0
11 - 10 = 1
12 - 10 = 2

Words to Know

equals—is the same amount or number.
minus—take away.
subtract—to take one number away from another.

Learn More

Books

Cleary, Brian P. *The Action of Subtraction*. Minneapolis: Millbrook, 2006.

McGrath, Barbara Barbieri. *The M&M's Subtraction Book*. Watertown, Mass.: Charlesbridge, 2005.

Murphy, Patricia J. *Subtracting Puppies and Kittens*. Berkeley Heights, NJ: Enslow, 2008.

Web Sites

Max's Math Adventures
http://www.teacher.scholastic.com/max

FunBrain
http://www.funbrain.com/brain/MathBrain/MathBrain.html

Index